REP
YOUR
ST🎯RY

TRUE STORIES OF FAILURES AND
SUCCESSES TOLD BY ELITE ATHLETES

JAY HERNANDEZ

PRAISE FOR
REP YOUR STORY

Every page of this great book features one inspirational tale after the next. First-hand accounts from larger than life superheroes offering lessons on how to overcome daily obstacles, both big and small. The best part is, while they are talking about their own experiences, there's something for everyone here to draw from and use as motivation. A great read.

Ariel Helwani
Combat Sports Journalist

Jay writes the way he lives his life–curiously, authentically, and intentionally. This book is an expression of his thirst for learning and his heart for others by sharing what he's learned. For anyone seeking improvement, it's a must read.

Amanda Butler
Former Women's Head Basketball
Coach at Florida and Clemson

Life will always be a combination of successes and failures, but how we handle them is what truly defines us. This book captures that perfectly at the absolute highest levels. It's really an inspiration for not only how to deal with whatever challenges life throws at you, but also how to become a better person in the process.

Omar Jimenez
Emmy Award-Winning CNN
Correspondent

For speaking engagments,
please reach out to Jay at
repyourwork@icloud.com

Rep Your Story
True Stories of Failures and Successes
Told By Elite Athletes

Author: Jay Hernandez
Editor: Taylor Brien
Proofreader: Griffin Mill
Cover Design: Nicole Wurtele
Interior Layout: Michael Nicloy
Author Photo: Nathaniel S. Butler,
                     NBAE via Getty Images

All athlete images are courtesy of and have been approved by the individual athletes.

ISBN: 979-8-9881891-6-9

PUBLISHED BY CG SPORTS PUBLISHING

AN IMPRINT OF
NICO 11 PUBLISHING & DESIGN
MUKWONAGO, WISCONSIN
MICHAEL NICLOY, PUBLISHER
www.nico11publishing.com

Quantity order requests can be emailed to:
mike@nico11publishing.com

Printed in The United States of America

DEDICATION

Rep Your Story is dedicated to the best starting 5 I have ever been a part of—and that happens to be my family. It's dedicated to my wife Allison who always inspires me to be great by how special she is in every facet of life. It's dedicated to my children, McKayla, Michael, and Morgan for giving me purpose and drive each day to be my best. They remind me that having fun and taking it seriously don't have to be separate entities.

I am so grateful that you all have been a part of this journey. I love you all so much.

TABLE OF CONTENTS

FOREWORD
TOBIAS HARRIS
BASKETBALL PLAYER

Long before I played my first game in the NBA, I was just a kid from Long Island, New York, trying to make a name for myself. I was introduced to the author, Jay Hernandez, as a teenager. He had a basketball training business and my father heard about his unique player development methods and figured it was worth trying. The training was special and we forged a strong bond over the years. I entrusted Jay to guide me through the pre-draft process and set up my entire workout schedule. In the 2011 NBA Draft, I was chosen 19th after one year at the University of Tennessee. I continued to work with him after I got drafted to prepare me to perform against the best players in the world.

In February of 2013, I was traded from the Milwaukee Bucks to the Orlando Magic and was afforded the opportunity to play right away. I was able to showcase all the work I had put in. Jay would always say, "Rep your work," to me after workouts. He wanted me to represent all the hard work I had put in and apply the skills I developed in games. I went from averaging 4.9 points per game in Milwaukee to averaging 17.3 points per game in the last 27 games of the season in Orlando. Finally, my work ethic met an opportunity, and I was able to capitalize.

There are many times when athletes get opportunities, and they fail after years of hard work in that pivotal moment that they were working towards. We have all been there. The best athletes learn from their mistakes; they are fueled by their mistakes and sometimes a failure can even develop confidence that propels them to future success. Another phrase Jay would use in training sessions was, "Make it ugly." He welcomed mistakes and I welcomed trying to find my weaknesses. I was finding them before the competition could and it came with some frustrating hours that turned into rewarding ones. He wanted that perfection wall to be shattered. Players should be celebrated for pushing past their limits and need to realize that they aren't going to be perfect learning a new skill. Failing was, and still is, a big part of the ultimate success. I was just as excited to read the "Rep Your Fail" section of this book because most people only remember the successes but, like myself, all these athletes grow most from the tough times.

Being able to read about the success and failure moments along with the paths of these athletes is the perfect complement to each other. It has me really reflecting on trying to pinpoint the "Rep Your Work" and "Rep Your Fail" moments throughout my career. I know each reader hearing from the Greats will realize that they have more in common with them than they realized. *Rep Your Story* will have anyone inspired to keep striving to reach the top in whatever field they choose.

For more information and behind the scenes content on Tobias Harris, scan this code:

www.repyourstory.com/featured-athletes/#harris

INTRODUCTION

*"The most dangerous person over the
course of time is the one who
is constantly improving."*
– Jay Hernandez

It is with great gratitude and some disbelief that Tobias Harris wrote the foreword for *Rep Your Story*. I am grateful because the young boy I met, trained, and coached is still a part of my life but now we are friends. Tobias has 13 years of NBA experience and throughout his professional life has been an integral part of social activism, charitable contributions towards education, and entrepreneurial endeavors that provide jobs in various communities. I could tell several stories about Tobias, and at some point, I will have him tell either his Rep Your Work or

Rep Your Fail moment. The reason I asked Tobias to write the Foreword was because he lends credibility as an elite athlete as well as the authenticity needed to set this book off properly. I know first-hand what it took for Tobias to not only get to the NBA, but excel in it. His preparation, work ethic, and confidence are just a few of the reasons why he has tripled the average playing career of an NBA player. It is a true blessing that my first NBA job reconnected me with Tobias and afforded me the opportunity to coach him at the highest level.

What I saw from Tobias at the NBA level was great professionalism and someone who had his own thoughts on basketball from his experiences. I had my experiences as well from training so many different types of players, but being in the NBA was new. I had to learn new terminology, go from running a business to being a part of one, and having to move away from my home. Having Tobias in Orlando helped because he got me acclimated to being in a new city, to what to expect during the season, and gave me credibility with the players just like he is doing in this book for the readers. We now had a chance to work together every day, year-round not just in the off-season. I was a part of a team, so I had to make sure that the skills he had worked on were matching up with what we were doing on court. I also had to make sure that he was not limited to only what the team was doing because coaches change, systems change, and Tobias, being so young, still had a lot of room to grow. Those formative years for both of us as professionals have paved a path that I know both of us can be proud of. We can be proud because none of it came easy, a lot of it came from sacrifice, failures, and doubts, yet we persevered and found fulfillment in the pursuit of being better in every way. That is why I always say the most dangerous person over the course of time is the one who is constantly improving.

I take a lot of inspiration from people and their stories so being able to write this book allows me to continue to inspire others to dedicate themselves in whatever field they choose. *Rep Your Story* embodies what it means to live your life without training wheels. Going for what you want can be scary, lonely, and, at times, unforgiving. I wanted to share the successes of four athletes after years of struggle in the Rep Your Work section and the failures of four athletes who are known for their successes in the Rep Your Fail section. It's the perfect balance of the highs and lows that everyone experiences in life. Rep Your Work moments and Rep Your Fail moments can happen at various stages of one's career and will happen multiple times.

My career-changing moment came in 2014 when I got an opportunity to coach in the NBA. The coach for the Orlando Magic at the time, Jacque Vaughn gave a chance to an entrepreneur from New York. I would have to figure out how to make it work. I had to talk to my wife Allison, who was not prepared to move and was a tenured teacher in New York– which is a coveted position to have. Allison and my three kids, McKayla, Michael, and Morgan were happy, and we had an incredible support system around us. I was offered a 2-year deal. I had to make the tough decision to go to Orlando on my own to make sure that being an NBA coach was what I truly wanted to be before I uprooted my family. I had to take a leap of faith that this opportunity was presented for a reason, and I wanted to have no regrets years later for not seeing what could come from it. I always took pride in being an example to my family and the players that were a part of my program. It was time to create a different chapter in my career and see if I had what it took to Rep My Story. My family moved out to Orlando in my second year and supported me every step of the way. I have accrued 10 years in the NBA, and I am still enjoying the process, learning, and repping to the best of my ability.

During my time running my business which developed the skills of amateurs all the way up to the pros, I realized that working on the mental side was just as important. Analogies and affirmations always resonated with my players. A specific quote would trigger the type of action or mindset I was looking for. Stories always connected the analogies, affirmations, and quotes I was using during a session. That is why this book was so much fun to write and will be so valuable to each reader in one way or another. Each reader will be armed with stories that they can use in any field. These stories let people know that they can fight through adversity, that they can keep going even without the support of those closest to them or that one moment can make all the difference in the world.

This started as a compilation book of hope for not only the reader but for me. I listened to each athlete and started to write; I realized that the hope I was looking to provide morphed into something more tangible. There are ways to approach doubts, struggles, and failures that will look to others like optimism but is rooted in reality. The reality of the Greats is that they understand what they need to do and will be disciplined enough to not get distracted. The plan is the plan, the process is the process and, because of this, all eight athletes that are featured were completely invested. Giving up became harder than to keep trying against what looked like insurmountable odds at times. Elite athletes are revered and cheered, as well as hated and booed, but no matter what, they should be respected. They perform without a safety net and every action/reaction comes with a result that is tied to years of hard work and preparation.

I have been able to witness some of the best athletes in the world train as well as compete from an arm's length distance. I have learned how various athletes learn, how they receive coaching, and how they get ready for competition. Each athlete is different and needs to be worked with in a way that they understand and can apply to reach optimal success. What motivates, resonates, and helps players remember will change. That is why I have tried to share the stories of people from different backgrounds and upbringings as well as very different sports cultures. Whether an athlete is competing as an individual or in a team setting there are plenty of moments where each person must decide what is most important to them professionally. They must approach each day with specific intent to be the best. These athletes are extremely candid about what their moments were and why. It is all written out in their own words based on their experiences and that is why it is so impactful. My objective is that you can always reference this book when you have doubts and realize that you are not alone. If you stay committed then you will be able Rep Your Story just the same.

Visit the Rep Your Story website:

REPYOURSTORY.COM

Instagram:

@REPYOURSTORY

X:

@REPYOURSTORY

PART ONE

REP YOUR WORK ATHLETES:

CHRIS WEIDMAN

MYLES JONES

NIC LAMB

CHRIS ALGIERI

REP YOUR WORK:
CHRIS WEIDMAN
Mixed Martial Artist

"I wanted to maintain that positive self-talk and confidence from that walk-in to the moment we touched hands. It was very hard and stressful. It was years in the making of constantly winning those self-talk moments."

C hris Weidman is one of the most highly regarded champions that has ever fought in Mixed Martial Arts (MMA). He has fought some of the best fighters/ champions the world has ever known and won. His biggest challenges and successes came under the Ultimate Fighting Championship (UFC) banner. The UFC is considered the premier MMA promotion with fighters coming from all over the world. Chris hails from Long Island, New York, in a town called Baldwin, and this is where Chris would establish himself as a standout wrestler. He went on to attend Nassau Community College and then committed to Hofstra University where he would attain All-American status. Chris "The All-American" Weidman would become how he got introduced to the crowd before his fights.

To make the jump from wrestler to fighter, Chris needed the guidance of former UFC Welterweight champion Matt Serra, who defeated Georges St-Pierre in one of the biggest upsets of all time, and Ray Longo, who trained some of the best fighters in the world. Chris was such a good wrestler that learning another ground fighting style like Brazilian Jiu-Jitsu (BJJ) felt natural to him. Chris would learn how to not only control fighters on the ground but would learn how to submit them with various choke techniques and leg/arm attacks. Chris would also learn how to defend against such attacks. This is where Matt Serra is a master and would sharpen the blade for Chris in this department. Longo's strength lies in teaching and training fighters to be able to fight on their feet which is also known as stand up. Stand up is inclusive of being able to use all the weapons that are allowed while standing up, like punches, kicks, knees, elbows, and clinching (grabbing and controlling technique). To be an MMA champion, one must be great at blending a variety of martial arts so they can easily flow through techniques. Although Matt Serra was known for BJJ, what helped him secure the championship versus Georges St-Pierre was how he was able to handle himself on his feet. With Chris' pedigree in wrestling, Longo knew Chris had what it took to be a champion because of his toughness, discipline, and dedication. Chris had the physical tools but in MMA those characteristics that Longo noticed will take you a lot further.

Chris was finding it hard to get matched up because of the team he trained with, and wrestlers are a nightmare to fight against because they can usually control where the fight goes. On top of fights being hard to get, Chris also had concerns from his family and his wife, Marvi, about making the transition from wrestler to fighter. In Chris' first fight he didn't throw a punch or kick. He wrestled, he took his opponent down, and used his Brazilian Jiu-Jitsu to submit him with a rear-naked choke. Imagine going into a fight where the opponent has trained to violently defeat you, but you choose to win in a fashion that makes your family comfortable? Well, that is what Chris did but unfortunately his path to legendary status would not come so easy going forward.

Chris was not making any significant amounts of money from his fights and had injuries that sidelined him, one of which he needed to have surgery for on his hand. To date, Chris has had over 30 surgeries throughout his career. He managed to overcome all of this, in addition to losing his home because of tropical storm Sandy, and still stayed the course. He had his doubts, as did his wife Marvi, but Longo talked to Marvi and told her what Chris could financially make in the UFC once he got in and that he believed he could become a champion. Marvi believed what Longo was telling her and they decided together that they would go after this dream.

Chris finally got the break he was lookng for when the UFC called. He jumped at the opportunity and took the UFC by storm, starting a perfect 9-0. He was looking to challenge who was widely considered the best fighter on the planet, possibly the best fighter of all time in Anderson "The Spider" Silva. Silva was not only knocking his opponents out, but he was making it look effortless. He looked like he was having fun in the Octagon, at times taunting his opponents, trying to infuriate them and bait them into trying to fight his type of fight. Nine fights didn't seem like quite enough experience to face a great like this, but Chris and his team were confident that his style and ability could get the job done.

CHRIS WEIDMAN
REP YOUR WORK MOMENT

I was 9-0 and fighting Anderson Silva, the greatest of all time and undefeated in the UFC. There weren't too many who believed I could get it done. I knew and I truly believed that I could beat him. The second I got into the sport I knew that I had never really accomplished my goals in wrestling. I wanted to be a national champion and an Olympic champion, and I always fell short. When I got into Mixed Martial Arts (MMA) Anderson Silva was already the champion. I always envisioned myself being able to fight and beat him. When I was fighting guys on the local scene and lower-level UFC guys, it wasn't about just fighting them, it was about getting ready to fight the best. My chance to fight him came relatively quick in terms of the number of fights I had but it didn't feel that quick in terms of all the ups and downs that had occurred.

It was important when going against Silva to not let the moment get to my head because he had beaten so many guys mentally before they even got into the Octagon with him. We had guys in training camp emulate his style. We brought in Stephen "Wonderboy" Thompson, who had a similar fighting style to Anderson. He helped me a lot. We also had southpaw boxers from New York that we used, so I felt very prepared. I had guys taunting me in the room while training. I wanted to maintain that positive self-talk and confidence from that walk-in to the moment we touched hands. It was very hard and stressful. It was years in the making of constantly winning those self-talk moments. When the doubts came in, not letting them settle there. Constantly beating them out with positivity and not losing. So, walking in there against Anderson Silva, I was very confident.

Silva didn't do much to me except for leg kicks to be honest. I was pressuring Silva. He started putting his hands down and playing the games. As much as I was prepared for it, I was just like, "I can't believe this motherf***er is doing this to me right now. Are you kidding me? You trying to play me like that?" I was trying to remain calm. Punch him, don't let him punch me. Walk forward. I expected to just submit, him to be honest. Take him down and submit him.

In the first round, I took him down and had success with ground and pound. I hit him with a really good shot on top where I rocked him, so I went right into a knee bar attempt then I turned it into a heel lock attempt, which was really a risky move on top. The reason it is risky is because if he gets out, he's either on top or back on his feet. I didn't care, I wanted to finish him. I went for it, he eventually got out and we were back up to our feet. I won the first round. There were a lot of antics of him with his hands down and stuff like that.

Longo (Weidman's Striking Coach) gave that infamous speech between the first and second round. "Punch a hole through his f***ing chest!" This instruction was technical because Silva would move his upper body a lot, not his legs. So, when he would put his hands down against the other fighters before me, he let them punch him with their best shot. Then, he would mentally break his opponents by eating their best punch. So, if you get punched through the chest, it gets your range in place so you can come up to the head. Next thing you know, Silva was taunting me, and I just had enough. I was like, "Bro you're not doing anything, I'm doing everything so shut the hell up." I thought to myself, "I'm not going to stop punching until I knock this f***ing guy out." I got pissed, which I'm not supposed to. I should've maintained my calmness. I just had enough. It worked out. I just went all out. Big right hand, threw a left hook, missed a right cross, came back with a backfist with that same hand and then a left hook. He did not see the left hook coming. That dropped him. When he dropped, I was like "holy crap." I pounced on him and started dribbling his head like a basketball until the ref pulled me off. I went nuts. I was still pissed. I was cursing at him for disrespecting me. He chose the wrong one.

It was a culmination of the feeling of not only beating Anderson Silva but knocking him out. A guy who no one has ever knocked out before. Since I was a little kid, I set out all these big goals that I never accomplished. And here I am, I finally did it at a sold-out venue on international fight week at MGM, Las Vegas. I was 28 or 29 years old and managed to capture my Rep Your Work Moment by knocking out the greatest of all time.

For more information and behind the scenes content on Chris Weidman, scan this code:

www.repyourstory.com/featured-athletes/#weidman

REP YOUR WORK:
MYLES JONES
LACROSSE PLAYER

"I had to decide, do I just keep the same work ethic, continue to push it to the edge and see what happens, or should I just do my thing in practice and focus more on school? I decided to keep pushing."

Myles Jones is a superstar in every sense of the word. He is one of the most feared and skilled mid-fielders to ever pick up a lacrosse stick. However, you may not have heard of him because he plays Lacrosse. The sport is growing because of the Premier Lacrosse League (PLL), which was started by the Rabil brothers (Paul Rabil is one of the best lacrosse players ever). The PLL has secured major sponsorships deals and has done a good job with its visibility on television and through social media. Unfortunately, the stars of the PLL aren't making close to what the stars of some of the other professional organizations are—but that doesn't mean one won't see the same type of grand skill and athleticism. If you watch Myles play, then you know he has that "It Factor." At 6'5", 260 lbs, if you saw Myles in the airport, you could confuse him with a power hitter in the MLB, a tight end in the NFL, or small ball power forward in the NBA.

Someone with Myles' size, skill, and agility are hard to duplicate for his position on the lacrosse field. This is why he is a 5x All-Star and one of the faces of the organization. He grew up playing basketball and football and he has stated, "Lacrosse is the perfect blend of both sports." Players must decipher either zone or man-to-man coverages and players like Myles are defended by the best defensemen, and at times will be double-teamed to try and stop their effectiveness. The offense has specific sets, there is a shot clock and coaches have installed a free-flowing motion with cuts and spacing just like the NBA. Professional lacrosse players are equipped with mouth guards, helmets, shoulder pads, and thick gloves. They get slashed by the stick and crashed into all while trying to skillfully pass, make moves, and change angles without losing possession of the ball. The game is as skillful as it is physically intense. This is the height of a sport that was originated by Native Americans.

Myles started playing in the 6th grade because his friends were playing. At first, he wasn't good at the game. Unlike some kids who quit when they aren't initially good at something, Myles wanted to prove that he could become great at lacrosse. He had some natural talent when it came to playing basketball and football, but adding a lacrosse stick and adding a new rule set would extend his timetable for success. He never ducked a challenge, and he found the fun in improving his skills. This is something that would become a staple of his not only on the lacrosse field, but off of it as well.

By the time Myles finished high school, he was an unguardable force who had earned All-American honors. His devotion to the sport and his academics drew the attention of the Duke University coaching staff. Myles accepted a scholarship to play for Coach Jon Danowski. His honors got even better in college where he became a three-time All-American which included two, first-team selections. He was also considered the top midfielder in the country by winning the L.T. j.g. Donald MacLaughlin Award.

Myles was able to lead his team to two National Championships during his 4 seasons there from 2013-2016. It would be a good assumption that one of these championships would be his Rep Your Work moment, but Myles chose a specific game before securing his second championship that propelled his career and set the stage for what was to come.

MYLES JONES
REP YOUR WORK MOMENT

I always tell this story and I think it's good for young kids. Everyone has their moment when it clicks. All our superiors told us about staying the course and all those cliches we hear as athletes. In my freshman year, I was just a kid who had small goals. I just wanted to play and make an impact in every game. Score a goal here, get an assist there. I came to Duke, and I started to get playing time right away. I got hurt in the middle of my freshman year. It was a hamstring injury that nagged me for a little bit. I ended up having a good year for a freshman and we won the National Championship, which I was pumped about. I got a lot of experience my freshman year.

My moment came as a sophomore in college. Coming into my sophomore year, we had three All-Americans graduate from the championship team. They all played midfield, so I knew it was my time to step up and I'd be the guy the team would look towards. There was another sophomore, Deemer Class, who played a lot with me when we were freshmen and was expected to be the star along side of me. We had an attackman, Christian Walsh, who transferred to midfield and had a lot of experience in a lot of playoff games and Final Fours. We thought we'd be one of the better midfields in the country.

When you're young, it really matters what the media writes about you. ESPN's *Inside Lacrosse Magazine* rates the top units for each position in the country every year. I got excited about them posting the midfield units in the preseason because I thought we'd be up there. When the list came out, we realized we weren't on that list. It listed the top 10. They had Virginia and Princeton, but not us. We felt a little bit disrespected. In hindsight, now that I'm a lot older, I know the list didn't mean anything. At the time though, it mattered and fueled us heavily. When we were left off the list, we started working even harder. We really got after it in practice. Our coach, Jon Danowski, took notice on how we were overexerting ourselves. He pulled us to the side and asked us, *What's wrong?* Coach D is very laid back and funny. He studies his guys, and he could tell we were on edge for no apparent reason. We didn't tell him that they didn't rank us and continued to train just as hard.

We got into the nitty gritty of the preseason. I wasn't playing horrible, but I wasn't playing well enough to my own standards. I was on pace to have a better year than my freshman year, but that wasn't good enough for me. Our coach always preached extra work outside of practice to get better because everyone is going to practice. He wanted us to set ourselves apart. We practiced five days a week and I committed to being on the practice field 30 minutes before practice and 30 minutes after practice. I figured if I could do that consistently, then that's five extra hours of work per week. I felt like I started to play better in practice. I could feel myself getting better and more confident in my skillset. The problem was I didn't feel like it was coming to fruition in the games. The stats were only a little better than my freshman year, if better at all. I took a hard look in the mirror. I thought about how I was at one of the best schools in the country that people would die to come to. I had to decide, do I just keep the same work ethic, continue to push it to the edge and see what happens, or should I just do my thing in practice and focus more on school? I decided to keep pushing. A couple weeks went by, and I still didn't see the improvement on the field. Coach pulled me aside and said, "We are seven games into the season, and you have 13 points." That's all he said. He knew I could do better, and I knew I could do better. I asked myself, "Why is it not happening?" We were winning as a team, so I couldn't feel bad for myself since we were achieving our team goals. I got on myself and I kept grinding.

I can close my eyes and still picture this whole game. We were playing against Virginia and Chris Lapierre, who was just on the cover of a lacrosse magazine as the biggest and baddest defensive midfielder in college lacrosse. He was supposed to be *that guy* on defense. He guarded the opposing teams' best midfielders and neutralized them. At this point, I've been working hard, so I knew that this was going to be a big game. It was always a big game against Virginia. They came out hooting and hollering. They thought they were going to beat us. They took us a bit lightly. The first play of the game came, and I got the ball. I remember it like yesterday. I had been working on shooting with my left hand because teams forced me left. I ran down the left alley and shot the ball on the run. It was one of my top three favorite goals of my career. I stuck it in the corner and the ball came out like four yards. For a half-second, everyone on the field was shocked. They knew I was right-handed, athletic and sort of predictable. So, people haven't seen this version of me before. After that, I scored another left-handed goal on the run where the other team realized they had to change their scouting report against me.

The Virginia game changed everything for me. I was able to do whatever I wanted. If teams forced me left, I could score with my left hand. If teams double teamed me, I found

open teammates. Before I knew it, I went from
seven games and 13 points to 50 points in the
ten games in the latter half of the season. I
ended the season as an All-American and we
won another National Championship. I like
to tell this story and let people know that I
had the opportunity to sit back and see what
could have happenened. I didn't. Instead, I
decided to put my head down and go get it. I
came back as the baddest dude for my junior
and senior year. I had a couple of the greatest
seasons in college lacrosse history garnering
Atlantic Coast Conference (ACC) player of the
year both seasons.

I think that seeing the reward from my
hard work became my visual from that point.
It really became all I knew. I knew that if I did
something physically with the right mindset,
I'd get the reward I wanted. Not only have
I really adopted that in terms of my athletic
career, but also with everything I do now.
Even today, when I'm working in real estate,
I see that preparation and hard work gives me
the results I want. When I go into each week,
I know I must do the dirty work in order to be

successful.   That is why I chose this to be my Rep Your Work Moment.

For more information and behind the scenes content on Myles Jones, scan this code:

www.repyourstory.com/featured-athletes/#jones

NIC LAMB
Big Wave Surfer

"Every time I'm in the ocean wearing a jersey it is a compilation of all the hard work I have done on land and in the water that has gotten me to that point and where I am today."

Nic Lamb, like the other athletes in this book, competes at the highest of levels. As a Big Wave Surfing champion, he surfs the equivalent of an eight-story building that shape shifts in ways that only a few people in the world can navigate. Making a wrong decision or move does not only affect a score but could mean a traumatic injury or even death. Unlike the other competitors in this book, Nic is working against nature's elements. Even though it's the same body of water for all the competitors, the wave and the ride are a completely different experience each time.

Surfing competitions are hosted based on weather patterns in different parts of the world that cause the biggest waves at different times of the year. Surfers have to be in shape, on call, and ready to travel across the globe when conditions appear to be ideal enough for teams to purchase their flights, book hotels, and get to the destination to compete. Some events that are projected on paper never go off. This is why surfers are a breed of their own.

The mentality of a Big Wave Surfer must be sharp, confident, and tough. The way they train is paramount to making sure that they are as ready as can be for all the variables they will face. Areas like strength, core, proprioception, injury prevention/maintenance, and breath are some of the keys to performing well when the time comes. Breath work and the right mental approach are needed for control, specifically in big moments. A surfer can utilize their breath to perform, or to survive just in case that surfer gets engulfed by a wave and is held under water for an extended period of time.

Thanasis Petrakis owns and operates Fresh Focus Sports, which is a company that films and documents the journey of athletes, coaches, and teams. Thanasis shot a 3-part documentary called "The Risk," where he followed Nic on his way to trying to win another championship. What Thanasis got to see, more than surfing, was the difficult side of recovering from injury, staying ready for competitions, as well as dealing with the disappointment of having tournaments canceled. Thanasis said that he got to witness Nic train, and "was very impressed by how dialed in he was with everything from rowing, squatting, sprinting, and balance-based exercises. No stone was left unturned."

Nic shows in his work that he wants to be ready when the moment arrives and truly lives the lifestyle. It hasn't always been easy for someone who grew up in the water. He started in the shadows of some of the giants of surfing, growing up in Santa Cruz, California. There were already a number of people he could reference from his hometown who had taken on Mavericks (an iconic big wave competition called the Titans of Mavericks hosted in Mavericks, California) and won. He wasn't trying to prove anything to anyone, he just wanted his opportunity. Nic still had his struggles and doubts about winning one of the major events, but it finally happened in Spain at the Punta Galea Challenge in 2014. He won this iconic event at the age of 26, ten years after he turned professional as a teenager.

Nic was able to showcase his skills, became a champion, and instilled a belief that he could become a multiple-time champion.

NIC LAMB
REP YOUR WORK MOMENT

A collection of moments throughout my lifetime surfing in the ocean at its gnarliest, at its biggest, at its most challenging all led me to my first Big Wave Tour win in 2014. It was in Spain at the Punta Galea Challenge and stands out as my Rep Your Work Moment. It was a far cry from when I remember my dad taking me out into head high surf when I was a kid, and it scared the s**t out of me. I'd cry saying I never wanted to go back. Growing up in Santa Cruz, California, was a melting pot of progression and big wave surfing that I was thrust into. By the time I was 12, I remember surfing waves up the coast from Santa Cruz that was a bigger adults-only surf spot. I just remember the looks of surprise on these grown men's faces when I was riding larger waves than them; it was bizarre. It's interesting now to reflect on how my psychology and growth changed over the years. It's like the trauma you experienced as a child you become attracted to as you evolve.

Our Big Wave Tour season starts in October and runs until March. It really depends on how many events they are able to run in a season because it is weather dependent. The athlete with the most wins or points at the end of the season takes the cake. Right now, we don't get many opportunities so when they are presented, we capitalize. It's not like other sports with dozens of games in a year. They say luck is when preparation meets opportunity. That's how I felt when I made it to the final of the Punta Galea Challenge.

I needed a 10 to win the competition. Getting a 10, especially at this moment, is like hitting a homerun in the bottom of the 9th in the World Series, except in our sport the stakes are beyond putting a ball past the wall, it's potentially life or death. There was only five minutes until the time was up for the competition to end. I not only needed to get a great score, but I also needed a wave. In the ever-changing algorithm that is the ocean one can only rely on probabilities based on years of data collection and pattern recognition to best position yourself in the lineup should another wave come. I did not know if another wave would come in time. I made sure I positioned myself should it come and knew I had the ability to execute if it did. The focus was on positioning for opportunity. To be honest, I was repeating, "Let's go," in my head to the ocean while remaining calm. It's all reaction at that point from compounding practice. The rest is outside your control so it's wasted bandwidth to focus on it.

The wave I needed came and I got the 10; I threw the arms up in the air, claimed it, and ended up winning the event. From there I won Mavericks and the Punta Galea Challenge again. That first big win did a lot for me. It proved something to myself that I believed long before anyone else. It validated the years of hard work and sacrifice starting back from that 12-year-old boy who rode the grown-up waves to the man who just showed the rest of the world my position and abilities. The biggest impact it had was it validated the upfront cost of years of dedication and sacrifice. After I won that, I thought to myself, *There's nothing I can't win.*

So, you ask, how much time and effort I put in prior to winning these events, winning in Spain? I have been surfing so long that I do not remember the first time I surfed on my own. Some people say you need 10,000 hours to become a master, I think it's 20,000, if anything growing. I mean, I put my whole life into every single event, every time I compete. Every time I'm in the ocean wearing a jersey it is a compilation of all the hard work I have done on land and in the water that has gotten me to that point and where I am today. I've won in the Pacific and the Atlantic Ocean. I've won airshows, shortboard events, and big wave events. It all comes down to process, focus on the process over events. You are rewarded in public for what you practice in private.

For more information and behind the scenes content on Nic Lamb, scan this code:

www.repyourstory.com/featured-athletes/#lamb

CHRIS ALGIERI
BOXER

"We were ready; we were ready for the fight in every way possible. We had a great game plan and knew what we had in front of us."

C hris Algieri has always been a competitor. He has had that fighter spirit and champion resolve from a young age. You could see it if you went to one of his wrestling matches in high school or during his kickboxing days, or in his backyard competing against his brother in just about anything. He was an All-State wrestling champ representing Saint Anthony's High School in New York. He set his sights on National's before a season-ending knee injury took him out of contention. He also won the Shotokan Karate Association title (SKA) which is the premier amateur kickboxing promotion before turning professional. As a professional kickboxer, Chris showcased his skills for multiple promotions and won numerous championships. Chris' extensive resume includes being the International Sport Karate Association (ISKA) World

Welterweight Kickboxing Champion and the
World Kick Boxing Association (WKA) Super
Welterweight World Kickboxing Champion.
Throughout Chris' life he has proven so many
people right but when he decided to become
a professional boxer, he would now have to
prove people wrong.

For the first time in his combat career,
he had been doubted and there was genuine
concern for his well-being. Keith Trimble,
who is one Chris' long-time trainers stated,
"Chris has that strong mind where he believes
in himself." Boxing doesn't seem that much of
a stretch from kickboxing but in their worlds,
they are at the opposite ends of the spectrum.
Most elite boxers start at a very young age.
They learn how to master angles, how to punch
and not get hit. For a guy like Chris, who was
used to fluidly mixing up his techniques with
his hands and feet, he would now have to limit
his attack to just using his hands. The way
you avoid punches in each sport is different.
A "roll" that is used in boxing to duck under
a punch would not be used the same way in
kickboxing because it could result in getting
kicked in the head.

Starting a boxing career at the age of 24 made Chris an immediate outcast in the boxing community. Most were waiting to see Chris get knocked out but that would never happen as he started off a perfect 10-0. The only problem was that Chris was making $5,000 to fight in sold out shows and was only getting one to two fights a year. Chris was making more money doing private lessons on the side and contemplated retiring. He made his intentions known to his manager and stated that he needed to be on big shows with a broader fan base so he could start making the money he deserved. His manager told him to sit tight and after just one additional fight, Chris was offered to fight Ruslan "The Siberian Rocky" Provodnikov for the WBO Welterweight Title. This was the opportunity he had been asking for. This was his chance to shock the boxing world and show his inner circle that his vision was correct. Most importantly it was time to realize the promise he made to himself to be a World Champion boxer. The opponent couldn't be any tougher or scarier. Chris was going to earn his championship the hardest way possible.

CHRIS ALGIERI
Rep Your Work Moment

My Rep Your Work Moment was winning the World Boxing Organization (WBO) Junior Welterweight title against Ruslan Provodnikov. It was on HBO, the Boxing After Dark main event at the Barclays Center in Brooklyn, NY. I was relatively unknown; I was not in the top 15 or even in the top 20 the fight prior. Before I got the fight with Ruslan, I was ready to retire. I guess that was on a Friday and Monday morning I got a call saying we have a fight with Emmanuel Taylor, who had a 17-1 record, with 12 or 13 knockouts. He had just come off two sensational knockouts on tv and the kid was #3 in the world. I didn't talk to my manager; I didn't talk to my trainer or my lawyer, and I said, "I am in." I didn't ask any details; in my mind, it didn't matter because this was my last chance. If I wasn't going to take this fight, then it's over. If I turn this down, then what am I really doing?

They named the bill the St. Valentine's Day Massacre because it was around Valentine's Day, and I was supposed to get killed. They put the show in my hometown because Emmanuel was from Maryland, and he didn't really have a venue with a fan base. I was very popular at the Paramount Theatre, which was in my home area of Long Island, NY, selling out the show every time I fought there. The fight drew ESPN cameras to the venue for the first time and we were the main event. As history wrote it, I fought him, and I won 8 of the 10 rounds pretty easily. I had out-boxed him; it was one of my favorite fights of my career honestly in terms of my performance against a very dangerous guy. Everyone kind of took notice that this kid from Long Island could fight. That was my coming-out party. He was #3 in the world, and he was supposed to fight Ruslan Provodnikov. When you beat the man who is supposed to fight the man then you get to fight the man.

It's funny; I saw my promoter the next morning after the fight and he asked me, "What do you think about fighting Ruslan Provodnikov for a world title?" We ended up working out a deal in terms of getting prefight money so I could go out to Las Vegas for a couple of weeks and train. It was a great camp! No stone was left unturned. We were ready; we were ready for the fight in every way possible. We had a great game plan and knew what we had in front of us. I think I was listed as a 15- or 20-1 underdog when the odds first came out. Word got back to Vegas that I could actually fight because a lot of people were coming to my camp to watch me spar and I was sparring with a lot of guys. By the time I fought Ruslan the odds were like 4-1. The odds had gotten so much closer just because we were getting so much quality work and we were not quiet about it. We were kicking ass and we were letting everyone know about it. It was finally time to fight, we had a great game plan, and I was super excited about it.

We were walking to the ring, and I was in the hallway and Paulie Malinaggi (boxing champion) grabs me and he goes, "Listen you can outbox this guy. You've got the length; you've got the speed. You've got the skills—just stick to the game plan." I had only fought primarily at the Paramount Theatre which has great acoustics, it's a music venue and it feels like there are 10,000 people when there's only a 1,000, maybe 1,500 in there. The Barclays can fit close to 10,000 fans and walking out there was something special. I walked to the ring with a flat brimmed hat very low by design so I couldn't see the crowd and I could only see the ring. I was laser focused and only thought about what it was I was supposed to do, what the game plan was. I got in the ring and then Ruslan got in the ring and my God. He was the boogey man of the division at the time, he was just one of the scariest dudes around. His nickname was "The Siberian Rocky", and he talked about how he ate moose liver as a kid to survive the harsh winters in Siberia.

In the first round I felt great. Everything was moving, working, my rhythm was good.

I was starting pretty fast, letting my hands go, and I wasn't having trouble finding him at all. I was surprised by how easy it was to hit him. I threw a funky hail Mary upper cut off the ropes and I cracked him on the chin, and I remember thinking, *like, really?* I threw that as a joke, and it landed. At this point I felt like I could speed up the game plan, that I could put some hurt on this guy early. Our plan was always to avoid the big shots early, out box him, weaken him with body shots, use the upper cuts to damage his eyes and his nose and then as the fight wore on, I could stop him. He cut a lot of weight and with him missing punches we figured he would get tired, and I could take advantage. I got greedy; I thought I could finish him sooner. I went to throw the same combination; a right uppercut and I was going to come back with a left hook, and he threw one at the exact same time. Mine landed, his landed bigger, *much* bigger. He's a really good puncher.

To this day I have never been hit like that. It felt like he punched a hole in my face, literally. It broke my orbital in 3 places, and it broke my nose in two places. I had 5 fractures from one punch. I had been down before in kickboxing, but never in boxing. I knew what to do, I knew to take my time, I knew to look at the ref, make sure I was coherent to let him know that I was good, ready to go, and focus on what's in front of me. At the same time my face felt so funny. It was a sharp pain with a radiating ache too. I had a sharp lightning bolt of pain coming from my tear duct all the way to my upper teeth. Then it radiated out to my whole face and head. I remember rubbing my face to see what was going on, but it was numb. I couldn't feel my skin or my upper teeth. It was weird because I had pain on the inside of my face. I didn't know what was going on, but I knew something was up. I got my standing 8 count; they rubbed my gloves off and next thing you know Ruslan is all over me. He was throwing punches and I couldn't really see him. Everything was blurry, I couldn't hit him because I couldn't see him, I couldn't defend myself because I couldn't see him, and I was still disoriented so I took a knee. Thank God I did. I went down on that knee, and it gave me time. I closed both eyes super hard and I just hoped that when I opened my eyes, I would be able to see again. And I did. Before the eight count was there, I opened my eyes, and I could see…and then I got up and my left eye worked. If I had one eye, then I could fight. The ref wiped off my gloves, we resumed the action and by the end of the first round I was boxing and boxing well.

I felt good and then I went back to the corner, and it was hectic. My corner was cool, Tim Lane and Keith Trimble were fantastic. My cut man, honestly, kind of looked at it like, *this is just a matter of time.* The doctor was trying to push my trainers out of the way to find out what the damage was. My trainers were trying to give me instructions. The doctor came in and I had a flashback of watching Arturo Gatti (former boxing champ) fight and having his eyes closed in so many fights and the doctor always asking, "How many fingers am I holding up?" The trick I learned from that is that you always say two whether you can see it or not, you always say two because they almost never hold up one. At that point I could still see a little bit even though they made me close my good eye and made me look out of the eye that was shutting. I got through that first one. Tim Lane said the most brilliant thing any corner man has said to me ever, "Hey baby you still got your lead eye, you're good!" He meant that my left eye is in front, and my right eye is in back since I am in an orthodox stance (right-handed boxer). If I keep my right hand up, I really don't need that eye. I can see his right hand coming; I can see his jab. My first perspective view is going to be from that lead eye anyway especially based on my stance. Right there my anxiety went out the window and I was thinking, *I'm good.* It was such an amazing cue by a coach to recognize that and the way he said it he was so calm, and it put me in a position where I was like, *cool, stick to the game plan.* We were going to win the fight with my feet and my lead hand anyway, *I just have to make sure I don't get hit in the eye anymore.*

The next couple rounds it was shaky because he was really coming on strong. He hit super hard, even the grazing shots that he did land hurt, but my whole mission was to protect the eye. For the most part, he couldn't find me. I kept the distance; I kept touching him and as the fight wore on, more and more rounds were going in the bank for me.

We were coming to the end, the eye was getting bad, it's just time, its gravity, there was blood in there and it was swelling, and my eye was completely closed by round nine or ten. Literally, in the 12th round I was blind in that eye completely. I think Teddy Atlas said it, "If you want out of a fight then say you can't see." It's quitting without quitting. The doctor came into the corner every round after the fifth because I was a mess. I told them I was doing great; I was feeling good—meanwhile my face was caved in, and I was in so much pain. They kept saying around round nine or ten that they were going to stop the fight one more round and I was like, "I am winning the fight, stop, he's not hitting me, I'm good, I am winning the fight, don't you dare stop this fight."

Going into the 11th, I was really in a bad place, I knew I was good, but my eye was shut, I was in so much pain and that was the first time where depth perception was really a problem. I couldn't hit him; I wasn't able to find out where he was anymore because I

couldn't tell how far away he was. In the 12th
I didn't have much left in the tank, my eye
was hurt, and I was just busy. I wear tassels
on my trunks and my shoes because it gives
the perception that you're moving a lot even
if you're not. I was thinking motion creates
emotion. I am going to woo the judges; I
am not really able to land anymore because I
can't really see him as much and I don't want
to commit too close to him because he is just
too strong. I spent that 12th round moving,
cutting in and out, tying him up, spinning him,
throwing punches and it *looked like* I was
doing a lot. The round ended and I knew I won
the fight, but I didn't think the judges were
going to give me the fight.

For me, I was sitting there, and I was
proud of myself because of what I had done, I
was also pissed at myself because I made the
mistake that injured my eye. They gave the
first score, and it was super wide for Ruslan,
and I thought they aren't going to let me win
the fight. Then they said *we have a split
decision,* and right there I knew I won. If one
judge could see I won the fight, then I knew I
would be declared the winner. The next two

judges had identical scores in my favor and the announcer says, "and the new!" The next thing I knew my eyes were closed, my hands were up in the air and this belt broke over my shoulder. The belt was heavy as hell, and it felt like the weight of the world just hit my shoulder. Our mantra during the camp was "and the new." We were screaming it all camp long, it's the first thing you hear when you beat the champ. I heard "and the new" and that was it, I was the World Champion, and I will be a World Champion forever.

It opened a new chapter, and it closed another one. It just shut everybody the hell up. I had so many people saying, "Where did this guy come from? Who are you? Why are you here?" I think a lot of fighters, especially through much of my career, were like this guy didn't come up through the amateurs with us, we don't know this guy, who is this guy? They would say I came out of nowhere. F-that, I didn't come out of nowhere, I was grinding for 15 years before I got there. I was working day in and day out and sacrificing and spending my money and living away from my family and missing every normal social thing you would ever do just to get to here. So many people would tell me, *You're a kickboxer, you're a karate guy, there's no way you can win a World Title in boxing.* Being a 15-1 betting underdog, Freddie Roach (Hall of Fame Boxing Trainer) telling everyone I was going to get knocked out in the first round and even my family would say, *What are you doing?* I have a master's degree; I don't need to do this. No one has ever fought in my family. I'm the first. I didn't grow up in a fighting family. I would just watch fights on TV and thought that I wanted to do that. My family was always like, *When are we going to be done with this? What are we doing here?* To me that moment just shut everyone up, and that is why it's my Rep Your Work Moment.

For more information and behind the scenes content on Chris Algieri, scan this code:

www.repyourstory.com/featured-athletes/#algieri

PART TWO

REP YOUR FAIL ATHLETES:

MICAH HYDE

SHASTA AVERYHARDT

ALEXANDER MASSIALAS

TIANNA MADISON

MICAH HYDE
AMERICAN FOOTBALL PLAYER

"That was my first eye opening failure because it was on such a big stage and the media became a part of it. People still bring it up and it adds fuel to the fire."

There is a sport in the USA that is known as much for its skilled positions as it is its brutal nature. It is called football. This is where men can get selected because of their 40-yard dash times, where they hit like trucks, and must maneuver like sports cars on the field. They also must have a brain and a work ethic that allows them to memorize extensive playbooks—not only for their own team but for their weekly opponents. More than any of the organized team sports there are a lot of incentive-based contracts and non-guaranteed contracts where players must consistently stay healthy and perform in order to get paid. If you are a player that can make it to a point where you hit double digit years of service and you are able to lock in multiple-year contracts, then you know you are doing something right. Micah Hyde has consistently been doing all the right things to go from a

5th round selection by the Green Bay Packers back in 2013 to one of the best players in the National Football League (NFL).

Micah started playing football with the kids in his community and quickly grew to love the sport. He also wanted to be like his older brother who was a standout player in his own right. At his brother's games you could find a little Micah running around and playing tackle football behind the bleachers. Micah did not just specialize in football, but he also played baseball and basketball. He felt that playing multiple sports helped hone his skills for football especially since he played so many different positions. He played quarterback, safety, kicker, punter, kick returner, and punt returner. He played mostly on the offensive end, but playing both sides of the ball would pay dividends when he got to college.

Micah was a highly touted recruit and chose to go to the University of Iowa. This is where his diversity of experiences would help him make the transition to the defensive side of the ball permanently. His college coach, Phil Parker, had a good reputation for putting players in positions that could help the team win games and optimize who they could become as a player. When he told Micah that he would be playing cornerback, Micah trusted him. After starting for the team for three years, he decided to enter his name into the NFL draft. Micah had a lot to prove after being selected 159th. He has certainly done that and then some. He was selected to the Pro Bowl in 2017 and is a two-time Second-team All-Pro selection. He is currently playing for the Buffalo Bills, a team that has expectations to win a Super Bowl.

It seems like Micah can do no wrong. He has been a standout athlete since his youth, has found his way in one of the toughest sports in the world, and is being compensated well for his efforts. The Greats know that getting to the top of their field always comes with trials and tribulations. They also know how to grow from them and exceed the version of who they were before they failed. Micah impressed his coaches and teammates enough to be playing meaningful minutes as a rookie in a playoff game versus the San Francisco 49ers. This is when he had his Rep Your Fail Moment which served as a reminder going forward to keep your eye on the prize and never take a moment for granted.

MICAH HYDE
Rep Your Fail Moment

This is my 11th year in the NFL. I've done a lot of great things and one day I'll be able to look back to see what I have accomplished. The number one thing that I continue to do is remember my failures and mistakes throughout my career. I'm a firm believer in not making the same mistake twice; I learn from my mistakes. I've made a lot of mistakes and had my failures. Once I got into the NFL, it became a whole different magnitude. There are millions and millions of people watching every week and it gets even bigger when you get to the playoffs.

In 2013, I was a rookie for the Green Bay Packers, and I was just trying to make a name for myself. I had that chance on January 5th, 2014, in a home playoff game against the San Francisco 49ers. It was in the fourth quarter in the Wild Card round of the playoffs. They had Colin Kaepernick at the quarterback spot at the height of his playing career and they had beaten Green Bay in the playoffs the year before.

It was a huge game. It was the coldest game on record I think, -3 degrees with the wind chill or something like that. The game was intense and there were key plays made and not made all game long. There were multiple lead changes with the game eventually being tied 20-20. This is when the key moment happened. Kaepernick rolled out, looking to pass it to his intended target, Anquan Boldin, who I was covering. He threw the ball flat. I jumped it, the ball grazed my hands, and I dropped the ball. That would've given us the ball with about a minute left on their 40-yard line. So, all we would have needed was a field goal to win. If I would've made that play, I would've become a household name in Green Bay—but I dropped it. The 49ers ran down the clock, got down the field to kick a field goal with no time left to win it. It was a tough catch to make, but that's what I do. I make tough catches. I always took pride in making tough catches. If that play happens another 300 times, I'm making it happen each time. It was just that one time, I took my eyes off the ball. I have no idea how it happened, but I have to live with it.

After the game ended, I was going down to the locker room and once I got in there, the media came up to me all at once. I was thinking, "What is going on? What did I do?" They immediately started bringing up the drop and saying if I made that play, we would've won. That was my first eye-opening failure because it was on such a big stage and the media became a part of it. People still bring it up and it adds fuel to the fire. I kind of like when people bring it up, weirdly, because I'm such a competitor. It makes me work harder. Back then, after that play happened, I got questioned the whole offseason. I realized that this is the business of the NFL and how much it all matters. It helped me work!

I had a really good second season. I had two punt returns for touchdowns and I made a lot of plays. That was my eye-opening moment to the business of the NFL and how fans get tied into it. That has made me a better player. I was in Green Bay for three more years after that happened and I was a good player. It wasn't until I got to Buffalo when I matured a little bit and had a family, that I realized how that mistake is still with me now and has made me a way better player. I stay locked into every play and every moment, so I won't feel that type of disappointment again. That is why missing that catch in my rookie season is my Rep Your Fail Moment.

For more information and behind the scenes content on Micah Hyde, scan this code:

www.repyourstory.com/featured-athletes/#hyde

SHASTA
AVERYHARDT
GOLFER

"I thought that I would feel instant criticism from those around me if I would have admitted I needed extra assistance to tighten up my game."

Shasta Averyhardt is a professional golfer. I could end the sentence there and Shasta would already be in the rare company of golfers who can claim the Professional Golfers' Association (PGA) or the Ladies Professional Golf Association (LPGA) status and that would be enough to write about her. There is so much more depth and scope when it comes to Shasta. Unlike some of the other major sports where athletes get paid to participate in a sport, golfers must pay to play and then have to perform at a better than average level just to break even. It is a high-stakes, high belief in one's game type of sport that is not for everyone. Sponsorships and winning are the only things that can prolong a career if an athlete is healthy enough to compete. Shasta most definitely created her own lane and has found her way over the years in order to be able to have the chance to qualify for major events and tour cards.

Shasta has defied the odds ever since she started playing golf at the age of seven. She learned from her dad, Greg Averyhardt. He worked for the county government as an Affirmative Action Officer and started playing golf to decompress with some friends after work. Shasta could be found running around with a golf club trying to keep up. With a small set of golf clubs, she would watch her dad and mimic his golf swing.

The sacrifices Shasta and her family had to make for her to be able to travel and pay to play is different than many other sports where there are more resources to help kids with the basic needs it takes to play a game. On top of that, Shasta grew up in Flint, Michigan, where they have had their share of elite athlete's but on the golf side there wasn't anyone Shasta could point to who had success. She was going to have to believe in herself like only trailblazers in any field can identify with.

Shasta was obtaining wins and seeing positive results in her sophomore and junior years of high school. These were all signs that the work being put in was applying to the course on competition days. She was focused on golf and trying to find ways to challenge herself to get better. She was ready for more and made a tough decision to go to another school for her senior year because they had a good golf program and she wanted to have a chance to win states. It takes a tremendous amount of commitment and sacrifice to leave the comforts of friends and familiarity. That sacrifice would pay dividends that would shape her life on and off the course.

Shasta earned a full scholarship to Jackson State University for golf. She has since been inducted into the Jackson State University Sports Hall of Fame for her accomplishments during her time there as well as after college. Historically Black Colleges and Universities (HBCUs) don't have a track record of producing PGA or LPGA tour members. Shasta was able to obtain an LPGA Tour card in 2011 which made her only the fourth African American woman to make the tour in its prestigious history. She was also the first African American woman to do so since 2001 when LaRee Sugg made the tour. Now, other up-and-comers have someone they can point to and know that they can become a professional golfer too. Shasta shares her Rep Your Fail moment in order for others to know that it's part of the game as well as part of the process. The failure that she had as a teenager is what fueled her ability to reach the top of her field.

SHASTA AVERYHARDT
REP YOUR FAIL MOMENT

A part of my story that most don't know is that I quit golf in middle school to play volleyball. My dad was fine with it at first but wanted me to return to golf. He told my mom he would get me a car when I turned 16 if I went back to golf. My mom relayed that message to me, and I agreed to go back, but I told my parents that I wanted a coach and I wanted to take it seriously. We found a man named Jack Seltzer, who coached a lot of the top women in the area. Around my sophomore year of high school, my game took a quantum leap. I was able to break par, I went to states, and then I won a couple of junior events. During my junior year, I ended up qualifying for some national events. A lot of the events are very expensive, and my family was very selective with our expenses. We didn't have the budget to go to many national events.

I made the decision that in my senior year I would transfer to an outer-county school because they had a really good golf program and a chance to win states. I wanted a state championship, not only individual, but a team one. It was tough to switch high schools, but I was focused on winning states. We won everything my senior year. We won the 9-hole matches and 18-hole tournaments. By the time we got to states, I was not playing well. We won as a team, but I did not win individually. That was disappointing because I wanted to win Miss Golf for the state of Michigan. I definitely put unconscious pressure on myself to win everything that year.

My final test was the individual state championship, which was the tournament I ultimately wanted to win, but I failed.

The morning of the first round of the state championship felt a bit uneasy. I knew how I was feeling in regard to my game and couldn't shake the lack of confidence before teeing off. The warmup was a blur, but I do remember teeing off on hole 1 as I was paired with Laura Bavaird, one of the top players in the state, who later became a friend. During the entire round, I felt unfocused, anxious, and doubtful, and it showed up in my opening round's score. That evening of the first round, I was distraught and embarrassed of how I performed.

I knew that my game needed some fine-tuning before heading to the state tournament but my fear of admitting my faults during a magical season would be too hard to endure. I thought that I would feel instant criticism from those around me if I would have admitted I needed extra assistance to tighten up my game. I guess the fear or maybe even ego got in the way. This lesson to ask for help took me a while to learn. Although I was highly upset with myself and my performance, I didn't pull the lesson from it right away until years down the road. Being honest with myself and not being afraid to speak up when I know I need help in any given situation is what I learned from not reaching my first big goal. The best overall lesson I learned is that this doesn't have to just be limited to sports performance and that is why this is my Rep Your Fail Moment.

For more information and behind the scenes content on Shasta Averyhardt, scan this code:

www.repyourstory.com/featured-athletes/#averyhardt

ALEXANDER MASSIALAS
Foil Fencer

"I was fencing like I had something to lose rather than trying to prove myself like I did when I was younger. I was more worried about what would happen if I lost a bout rather than just competing."

A lex was exposed to foil fencing at a young age because his father happened to be a 3x Olympian in the sport. His father, Greg Massialas, also owned and operated the Massialas Fencing Club which has produced some outstanding competitors. Greg was keen on having his son try other sports and didn't allow him to start training until he was seven. The focused training, the love Alex has for the sport, along with his athletic ability, all made it possible for him to make the Senior World Championship team at the age of 14. It was unprecedented, just like it was unprecedented for an 18-year-old by the name of Gerek Meinhardt to make the 2008 Olympic Team the year before. Gerek paved the path for Alex to see it was possible, especially since he was trained by Alex's dad, Greg. The doubts, the laughs from outsiders, and the roadblocks were not enough to stop the belief and determination Alex had to become the most decorated American athlete the sport has seen.

Foil fencing is one of the most intense one-on-one competitions that one can experience. It requires very specific skills, cat-like reflexes, technique, athleticism, ultimate focus, and strategy. Scoring is to 15 and you cannot win by two. There is a game plan going in, there are specific styles each athlete prefers but the best analyze, calculate, and adapt in real time in order to win the match. Alex has proven time and time again that he is a tough match-up for anyone in the world. At 6'3", and with over 15 years of experience that he has had at the world stage, he is in a category of his own. The other aspect that adds pressure to a highly stressful match is that an individual match that is won or lost could mean the difference in the team winning or losing an event or even medaling in the Olympics.

Alex has many accolades and honorary distinctions that would make the casual fan think that he has been destined for success and that there have been no struggles. He was the youngest male athlete at the age of 18 representing Team USA in the 2012 Olympics and he hasn't looked back. He earned an individual Silver medal and a team Bronze in the 2016 Olympics and was part of the team Bronze in the 2021 Olympics. That's three Olympic medals, but he has had his moments where he felt off, when he was losing, and had to figure out how to get back to being at his best. Alex's Rep Your Fail Moment is one that many athletes both young and experienced have felt at some point. As a freshman in college Alex tasted defeat many times and understanding what he needed to do to change the outcome helped propel his career to new heights.

ALEXANDER MASSIALAS
REP YOUR FAIL MOMENT

My failure moment was my freshman year of college. I started competing in foil fencing on the senior circuit at the age of 14. From that time up until my freshman year in college, my career in foil fencing showed growth and improvement; every year my world ranking was continually going up. I started out at 100-something in the World Rankings, then jumped to 60, then to 32. After the London Olympic games, I was ranked top 16 in the world. That's a very big benchmark for fencers because during the competition days on the World

Cup circuit, you're exempt from the first day of competition. You get a bye directly to the elimination round. Getting into that top 16 was a very proud moment for me because it made me feel like I had truly arrived on the scene. It would be an upset for someone to beat me at this point.

I committed to and attended Stanford University in 2012 on a scholarship for foil fencing. I was now competing as a student-athlete in the NCAA after competing on the world stage. In the first few competitions of the year, I really started to falter. It wasn't looking very good for me. I flamed out in the first three or four competitions in a row. I couldn't win a bout in the first round of the 64. Ultimately, that dropped my world ranking out of the top 16 and into the 20s or so. That was a demoralizing moment because I had just proved to myself that I could be in the top 16. Just as quickly as I got there, I had dropped out. That was a moment where fencers would get in their own head about it.

I give a lot of credit to my family for helping me keep my head on straight. My dad told me not to worry about my world ranking. He told me I could medal at any competition. I knew I had to change something; I knew something was wrong. But I didn't know exactly what it was. I think I relaxed a little bit after making the top 16. Initially, having the safety net of being in the top 16 held me back a little when I first got in. I was still training the same, but my mindset changed a little. I was fencing like I had something to lose rather than trying to prove myself like I did when I was younger. I was more worried about what would happen if I lost a bout rather than just competing. If you fence well, good things will happen. After getting a bunch of bad results in a row and falling out of the top 16, I went back to focusing on competing well. That was a giant wake up moment for me as far as my mindset was concerned.

I went into a competition in Korea at the end of the season before World Championships outside of the top 16. I was in the 20s or 30s. I knew I'd put in the work to be where I needed to be. I turned a horrible season into winning my first ever World Cup in Korea, which was a huge deal for me. I had only won Silver before, so this was my first time on top of the podium. The following weekend, I won a Bronze medal. That was my first-time medaling in back-to-back competitions. So even though this was my worst season through three quarters of the season since joining the senior circuit, I ended up turning it around into one of my most successful seasons to date. I ended the season top 10 in the world. I kept that consistency after that for years all the way until current day (2024) where I am sitting at #1 in the world.

That was my first Rep Your Fail Moment but would definitely not be my last. I had another rough season years later after the Tokyo Olympics. I was riddled with injuries; the season was shortened because of Covid protocols, and I didn't perform well at all. It was difficult to get into any kind of positive rhythm. What helped me was that I was able to recall that I had overcome this before when I was younger and less experienced. I am currently working towards winning Gold in the next Olympics in Paris, and I wouldn't be at this point of my career without growing from my failures.

For more information and behind the scenes content on Alexander Massialas, scan this code:

www.repyourstory.com/featured-athletes/#massialas

TIANNA MADISON
TRACK & FIELD

"I had no support as a reigning Olympic champion going into an Olympic year. I had a manager drop me as well. People in my inner circle were telling me it's time to call it quits. So basically, I got rid of a lot of people in my inner circle and rebuilt my team."

Tianna Madison is known by the sports world for the three Gold medals she was able to claim in multiple Olympics in track and field. Coming from humble beginnings, trained by her father, who was an accomplished wrestler (not a track star) in Elyria, Ohio, didn't bode well to create a college student-athlete, let alone an Olympic Gold medalist. Tianna's champion mentality, natural athletic talent, intellect, and persistence paid off not only for her, but also for America as well.

Tianna actually wanted to follow in her father's footsteps and wrestle, but her mom was adamant that she played another sport. The only other spring sport available at that time was track. Running for fun was a foreign concept for Tianna. Tianna signed up and once she started practicing, she started beating the boys. Once she realized that she was pretty good at it, it lit a curiosity, and she kept finding ways to improve in order to win meets.

Tianna kept finding meets to attend in order to find her weaknesses, address them, and work on them until they were gone. Tianna's dad, Robert Madison, would drive wherever, whenever to make sure Tianna could compete and got the visibility she was seeking from colleges. She ended up winning nine state championships in Ohio before her high school career ended. Tianna went to college for free, but it came in the form of an academic scholarship to the University of Tennessee after finishing her high school years with a 4.0 GPA. Her parents did not finish college, so this was an incredible moment for the family. Obviously, Tianna could have accepted a full athletic scholarship for her athletic efforts and accomplishments but being able to have a choice is something that Tianna has always taken pride in. She has been able to compete in different events in track and field and she has been able to create various opportunities in life because of the way she cultivates her many talents.

It is hard to see the train stopping, especially when it picks up a head of steam the way Tianna did once she had the resources to help her reach her full potential. The unfortunate part is that the train will eventually stop.

Sometimes the way the train stops or where it stops is not what was envisioned by the person or athlete when they thought of how things would end. Tianna's Rep Your Fail Moment will take you towards the end of her career and provide the most unique outcome and perspective that was written in this book.

TIANNA MADISON
REP YOUR FAIL MOMENT

If you've done all the work to prepare, you have to just be like, "F**k it, I'm here now." That's exactly how I am. In terms of my failure, it's very recent. It was in 2022, so a little fresh. I was actually the reigning Olympic champ in the Long Jump and the 4x100 relay from the 2016 Rio Olympics. That was a very interesting position to be in because I had a target on my back. I was 36 years-old. Nike tried to find ways not to pay me because I was considered old. My performance didn't say I was old, but Nike was telling me I was. It's tough not to take that personally as an athlete. Then there was the pandemic, and I had some health issues that took me out of the game anyway. The pandemic cancelling the Olympics worked in my favor because it allowed me an extra year to get back to being healthy.

At this point, Nike finally dropped me. I had no support as a reigning Olympic champion going into an Olympic year. I had a manager drop me as well. People in my inner circle were telling me it's time to call it quits. So basically, I got rid of a lot of people in my inner circle and rebuilt my team. It was a ragamuffin team of people who believed in me and cheered for me. I had a married couple who were World Champion bodybuilders working as my nutritionists so I could cut weight safely and sustainably. No one else in track and field had thought of that. I had a strength and conditioning coach that was a little outside of the box. My best friend oversaw my workouts and helped me execute them. Every day, we were grinding. The Olympic Trials were coming. Everyone was talking about the young girls that would be the breath of fresh air on Team USA. No one was talking about me anymore. I felt like Rocky. I was minding my own business and training. A couple weeks before the trials, I jumped a distance that I hadn't jumped in seven years in the long jump. I also ran the 100 in 10.9 seconds, which is an elite world-class time. To run under 11 seconds is elite. Finally, people realized I was back.

When I got to the trials, I didn't feel right. I was still being competitive, and I made it out of the first round and into the semifinal. I think I was the first one to not make the final. Jumping felt weird in the long jump. It was not a good situation, and I was embarrassed because that was the event I was the reigning champion in. It turns out that I was two months pregnant and didn't know it. So, I did all of my training and all of my cutting weight with that. I had this chip on my shoulder from people not believing in me from the beginning. I won World Championships at 19 as a surprise. Nobody was even at the meet for me because they didn't think I'd win. I had this chip on my shoulder throughout my whole career. I hate to lose, so I let myself be in that empty space for 24 hours.

In that failure of not making the team, I learned so much about myself. I learned that I was willing to take my body to the extremes. I went from 152 pounds to 130 pounds in a healthy way. I was able to be a positive role model for those women who have body-positivity issues, especially around being muscular. I enjoy lifting and I'm happy to show off my muscles to those girls. I was shredded *and* feminine. It's okay to be both of those things. I was able to model that journey in this defeat. You don't always have to find a silver lining when failing because sometimes it just doesn't work out for you. In this particular case, I learned so much about my capacity. It fueled me moving forward, not in sports, though because my baby most likely retired me. Now I know that I have the ability to do amazing things. I accomplished so much being pregnant. It made me think, *what else can I do*? I was a professional athlete for 16 years. My job is to learn how to bounce back from failure. This is the one failure that I don't have the opportunity to avenge on the track. This is the failure I wanted to share because I learned about the role of curiosity in your pursuit of personal greatness. You literally just have to wake up every day and ask yourself how much better can you be? Then do everything you can that day to answer that question. Once you do that, even if you fall short like I did, you can still get an answer to that question. You don't need external validation to answer that question. That is my Rep Your Fail Moment.

For more information and behind the scenes content on Tianna Madison, scan this code:

www.repyourstory.com/featured-athletes/#madison

CONCLUSION

*"No one who accomplished anything
great was ever considered normal."*

– Jay Hernandez

W hat an honor it was to write about
these extraordinary human beings
who challenge themselves in front
of fans, critics, and loved ones on a regular
basis. It is unfathomable to most people to
work towards something and be tested in front
of anyone who cares to watch. That is why
athletes are so highly regarded. They must
be of peak mind and body, and the cruelty
of it all is that sometimes that is not enough
to get the job done. Hard work is just the
price of admission. Champions have been
crowned for many reasons, and those who

have been defeated fall for many reasons as well. That is why it was so important to hear the perspectives of all eight athletes in this book. The one thing that reigned supreme was that they all believed they could be great even if the odds were stacked against them. They believed they could be great even when they didn't have the resources, or their closest supporters thought they were crazy. They believed enough to overcome doubt, to stay disciplined and dedicated to what they wanted most. There is nothing normal about the journeys these athletes had to take or how they go after what they want. That is why it's my belief that no one who accomplished anything great was ever considered normal.

The Rep Your Work features showed us that even the most decorated and celebrated athletes have had their share of heartbreak, struggle, and times where they wanted to quit. What kept them going was belief! Chris Weidman dealt with social pressures to get a "real job" after making no money, dealing with his house being flooded, and having some serious injuries. He was feeling like he couldn't win in life until he made the most of his chance in the UFC and became a great champion. Nic Lamb started surfing so young and loved what he was doing but winning a major big wave event had eluded him for some time. He believed that the right wave would come, and his skill would allow the judges to see him fit to be a champion. Chris Algieri was also dealing with the lack of confidence from his inner circle to make the jump from kickboxing to boxing. He was also making little money even though he was selling out shows and winning all his fights. He needed to advocate for himself and finally got the shot he was longing for. Myles Jones was dealing with trying to quiet the outside noise that said he wasn't one of the best players in the country and by trying to prove them wrong it tightened up his game. He finally figured out how to be present in the moment and let his work be applied in the biggest moment of his career up to that point.

The Rep Your Fail features are all athletes who have climbed the heights of their chosen profession, but at some point in their career they failed when it mattered most to them. Some of them failed and found confidence.

Imagine, lasting 12 rounds with Mike Tyson in his prime but losing a decision. It would be a badge of honor and you would feel confident going into any other fight after that. Some of the athletes who failed learned something that they could do better for next time. Some of the athletes used the failure as fuel to work harder or smarter and to keep that fire burning until next time. Either way, it was a belief that they had that allowed them to get back to work and make the necessary adjustments to win when the next opportunity arose. Shasta Averyhardt had her first notable failure in her senior year in high school that enabled her to make the adjustments in her training to be a better golfer in college and eventually as a professional. Tianna Madison can live with her failure because she knows what it took to get three Gold medals and pushed herself to train to get the same results even when there were circumstances working against her. Micah Hyde believed, and still believes, he has the best hands in the NFL. If he let the media, fans, or any other people shake his confidence after a key playoff game in his rookie year, then he would not have made it to the Pro Bowl or start for a team that has Super Bowl aspirations. Alex Massialas believed he could be the youngest male in the Olympics (and eventually win medals) even though he wasn't as physically mature as his competitors and lacked the experience. Failing to meet expectations after a world ranking was the reset he needed to find a way to become one of the most decorated U.S. foil fencers ever.

I believed in this book even before I ever started to type my first word. There was something pulling at me to keep taking notes, drawing logos, talking to family and friends about it until I realized during Covid that I had to get this process started. There were too many people losing hope and belief that they could set their sights on projects and careers in order to achieve greatness because of how the world shut down. There was a sense that it was all out of our control. *Rep Your Story* if nothing else will humanize the best of the best. We will all realize that everyone goes through the same range of emotions, but those emotions don't last, the work does. Those who believe continue to work and those who work continue to believe. Continue to appreciate not just the champion but what champion pedigree is all about. I believe in you because you are reading this, and you know what you have to do. It is time to Rep <u>Your</u> Story!

SPONSOR SPOTLIGHT:
WHITE ARK ENTERPRISES

W hite Ark Enterprises is the Title Sponsor for *Rep Your Story*. We wanted to connect with a company and a visionary who saw this not just as a book about elite athletes and their stories but a compilation book of inspiration. Everyone has a story, and Andres (Andy) Garcia has grown White Ark Enterprises based on the foundational principles he learned during his time playing basketball.

Andy grew up in a single-parent household as a kid and saw basketball as a way to provide for his family. He shined shoes, sold dresses, and washed dishes to make ends meet and would play basketball until the early hours of the morning. The combination of hustling on and off the court would pay dividends for him down the line. Eventually, Andy got the call to play in Mexico City where he would get to showcase his skills in front of a passionate fan base and against pro-level competition. He became a fan favorite because of his tenacity and his ability to shoot the ball with the best of them. He started to meet and get mentored by some of the most successful businesspeople in the region. They saw his work ethic and ability to connect with his coaches and teammates and knew that he could transition from playing basketball to running his own business.

He was able to do this alongside his brother Gustavo Garcia, growing a successful contracting business in part because of the relationships Andy fostered in Mexico City as well as the U.S. *Rep Your Story* was made for people like Andy who will keep striving to be the best no matter what obstacles are in the way.

Thank you, Andy, for your belief in the book and for your unwavering support.

Please visit www.whiteark.co for more information.

THANK YOU

Thank you to everyone who had a hand in making this book possible. Thank you to my family and friends for putting up with me for years talking about a book I wanted to write. A special thanks goes out to the individuals listed below for helping me with mentorship, setting up meetings, connecting me with athletes, transcribing, shaping the framework of the book, adding depth to the book, and more.

Cejih Yung

Mike Nicloy

Taylor Brien

Nicole Wurtele

Andy Garcia

Ron Douglas

Cierra Burdick

Thanasis Petrakis

Keith Trimble

Jon Diebler

Hernando Planells

Nick Barrotta

Daniel Roy

Maxwell Clevens

Adam Hoffman

A special thanks to the athletes who told me their stories and provided me the opportunity to share them with the world. If not for their willingness to open up about their lives I wouldn't have had the chance to write this book. You are all amazing people who have also accomplished greatness in your chosen field. I look forward to following you all and seeing more success to come in competition and in life.

Thank you to those who endorsed this book. I am a true fan of all of your work and the people you are. It is a true honor for you to take the time to read and support the book as well as support a first-time author.

Lastly, thank you to all of the players who I have ever had a chance to work with. To all of the players who listened, gave their all, and forced me to get better because they kept getting better.

ABOUT THE AUTHOR

Jay Hernandez has just finished his 10th season as an assistant coach in the NBA. He has been working with the best basketball players in the world helping hone their skills,

as well as scouting opponents and coming up with strategies to help the team win. He previously owned and operated Pro Hoops Inc. for 10 years, developing the basketball skills of athletes from amateurs to the pros. While playing college basketball for Hall of Fame coach Jay Wright at Hofstra University, Hernandez learned valuable lessons on leadership, accountability, and, most importantly, the mentality needed to be a great competitor and teammate.

Jay played basketball professionally for three seasons in Puerto Rico, and started training athletes while in college before he opened Pro Hoops Inc. He has seen what the barriers can be for players of all ages, backgrounds, and circumstances; and has narrowed down his coaching to a very specific formula: *Don't be afraid to make mistakes. If you aren't challenged, then you will be bored and won't improve. Getting better is forever, it's not a quick fix. Go apply what you learned and then do it all over again.* This led to him coming up with phrases, affirmations, and telling stories to cue the athletes, to make them believe, to continue to fight through obstacles, and to know that the athletes they looked up to have dealt with the same types of challenges.

Jay started an amateur career in Muay Thai in his 30s, where he learned all over again what it felt like to be a beginner, to be scared, and to find a way to be present in the moment. He realized quickly that he would need to

live within the advice he gave to his players:
In fighting, you can't have a mental lapse,
because it could mean getting hurt.

The appreciation Jay has had for training
and improving started at a young age and
carried into his time working with athletes.
His experiences as an athlete, as a trainer,
and as a coach allows him a great advantage
in being able to ask the engaging questions
that opens up the athletes to tell some of their
most impactful moments in their careers. Jay
wanted a book that included a wide scope of
athletes from major team sports to solo sports
who were all striving to be at their best when it
mattered most. It doesn't always work out that
way and that is the beauty in each story told.
Just like Jay's story, just like yours.

www.ingramcontent.com/pod-product-compliance
Lightning Source LLC
Chambersburg PA
CBHW082106140626
46553CB00018B/1312